What Do We Know About the Lost Colony of Roanoke?

by Emma Carlson Berne

illustrated by Stephen Marchesi

Penguin Workshop

For Dale, who loves history as much as I do—ECB

To my brothers, Louis and Dennis—not all who
wander are lost—SM

PENGUIN WORKSHOP
An imprint of Penguin Random House LLC
1745 Broadway, New York, New York 10019

First published in the United States of America by Penguin Workshop,
an imprint of Penguin Random House LLC, 2025

Visit us online at penguinrandomhouse.com.

Library of Congress Cataloging-in-Publication Data is available.

Printed in the United States of America

ISBN 9780593752081 (paperback)   10 9 8 7 6 5 4 3 2 1 CJKW
ISBN 9780593752098 (library binding)   10 9 8 7 6 5 4 3 2 1 CJKW

The authorized representative in the EU for product safety and compliance is
Penguin Random House Ireland, Morrison Chambers, 32 Nassau Street,
Dublin D02 YH68, Ireland, https://eu-contact.penguin.ie.

Contents

What Do We Know About the Lost Colony of Roanoke?

On August 15, 1590, an English ship called the *Hopewell* dropped its anchor off the coast of an island in the Outer Banks, near what is today North Carolina. The *Hopewell* had been traveling since March 20, and had finally reached the site of the English colony of Roanoke. John White, who was the governor of the colony, was aboard the *Hopewell*.

Three years earlier, he had sailed from Roanoke Island to bring supplies back from England. Now, after many delays, he had returned. He was eager to see his daughter, Eleanor; his baby granddaughter, Virginia; and the other English colonists again.

John could see the land from the deck of the ship and, even better, smoke from a fire. His family would be there, waiting.

Unfortunately, it turned out to be the wrong island. The next morning, John and the sailors loaded into small boats to row to the correct island. But even though Roanoke Island was so close that they could see the trees on shore, this short journey was dangerous. Waves rose and crashed along the shore, and the crew were in open boats. On the short trip, all the gunpowder, food, and bullets in one boat got soaked with water. Another boat turned over, and seven sailors drowned.

The rest of the crew was starting to wish they'd never agreed to take John to shore. They wanted to turn back. But John insisted they take him in. He hadn't waited three years just to turn back now.

On their second attempt that day, the boats finally reached shore, but darkness had already fallen, so John and the sailors anchored their boats, letting them bob on the water until morning. Through the trees, they could see the fire burning. They'd wait until morning to go ashore, they decided. Throughout the night, they blew a trumpet they had with them, sang English songs, and called out, but didn't get a response.

At last, morning came. As soon as it was light, John and a few companions set out. First, they investigated the fire. Just a natural fire, it turned out, probably started by lightning. No people were around.

Then John saw it. On a tree near the deserted shore, someone had carved three letters: *CRO*. A clue. But who had left it?

The village itself was empty, too. All the houses had been taken apart, and the colonists had built a sturdy fence of logs around where the homes had once been. John could tell by how much brush had grown up around the ruins that no one had lived there for a long time.

Then John saw another clue. On one of the fence posts, a word had been carefully carved: *CROATOAN.* Another sign. And perhaps, an answer.

CHAPTER 1
Life in Coastal Carolina

The people who lived in the coastal area of what is now North and South Carolina were part of the Algonquian, a group of Native communities who spoke related languages and shared cultural similarities.

A Secotan man

Under this large umbrella, smaller groups organized themselves into villages of one to two hundred people up and down the coast and farther into the mainland. These villages included Tramaskecooc, Croatoan, Aquascogoc, Pomeiooc, Cotan, and Secotan. Groups of villages were governed by leaders called *mamanatowick* (say: mah-mah-nah-TOW-ik), and within that system, each individual village was then governed by a *werowance* (say: were-WANTS).

For thousands of years before John White and his settlers landed on their shores, the Carolina Algonquian peoples had been living in what is now the eastern part of the mainland coast of North Carolina—loosely from present-day Albemarle Sound south to the Pamlico River. They also lived on the string of barrier islands now called the Outer Banks, including Croatoan Island, which today is called Hatteras Island.

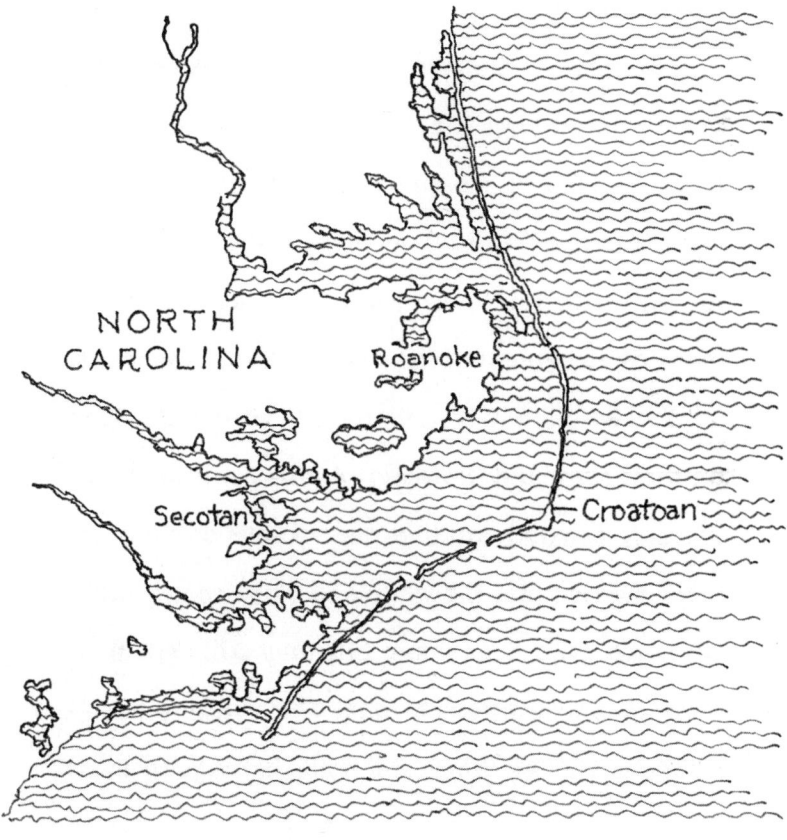

The Carolina Algonquians

By the late 1500s, anywhere from five to ten thousand people lived in settled villages up and down what is now the North Carolina coast and barrier islands.

European colonizers (people who take control of an area of land that is not their own) brought diseases such as smallpox with them when they arrived in the Americas. As disease spread through the Native populations of the Americas, it killed as many as 90 percent of them within a hundred years.

The Carolina Algonquians who survived stayed on their own land, however. As the centuries went by, they married and had generations of children. Some married into the white and Black communities who now lived near them, but they still kept their Algonquian traditions strong. Their culture hasn't disappeared. The group still holds heritage festivals and social and cultural gatherings called powwows. They fight to keep coastal North Carolina's land and water clean and protected from development to honor the land they have lived on for so long.

The Algonquian peoples of the coastal Carolinas were hunters, fishers, and farmers. The walls and roofs of their houses were built of wood and bark with woven mats that could be rolled and unrolled to let light and air in. Families slept on benches around the walls, and a fire in the middle kept the house warm. In the center of each village was an open space for meetings and religious gatherings, along with human-made ponds to collect freshwater.

The people hunted turkeys, squirrels, rabbits, bear, and deer, and gathered roots and nuts. They worked in their fields, where they grew corn, beans, pumpkins, sunflowers, tobacco, gourds, melons, cucumbers, and peas. On platforms above the field, people would take turns watching for animals who might eat the crops. At night, they cooked their meals over grills on outdoor fires or made stews or corn pudding. Special drinks were brewed from sassafras, ginger, and other herbs.

This land was braided with inlets, marshes, and rivers snaking in from the nearby ocean. The people who lived there fished in canoes made of single logs that were burned, scraped, and smoothed out. Some of the canoes could carry

as many as twenty people. They wove fence-like nets that they used to catch fish. During the spring and summer, they made trips to the barrier islands off the coast to fish in the deep ocean water.

The Carolina Algonquian grew plenty of food in the rich soil and tended their crops carefully. Their diet was healthy and nutritious. They made

Clay pot

beautiful, sturdy clay pots for cooking and storage; wooden dishes; and copper jewelry. They also made swords hardened with fire, willow bows, and reed arrows topped with fishbone arrowheads for hunting.

Across the Atlantic Ocean, though, life in England was very different. John White and other Europeans were part of a longtime system of colonialism that existed all over the world. Europeans at this time were beginning to send exploratory groups to almost every continent on Earth. They were looking for many things: shorter routes to countries with which they wanted to trade, gold and silver, and land for farming.

Even though living on these lands were

civilizations who already had been there for thousands of years, European colonizers moved onto land that was not theirs to settle. They believed they had the right to establish their own communities—colonies—on any new land they encountered, especially in North and South America and the Caribbean. While some British settlers were looking for freedom to practice their own religion, those from Spain and Portugal were more interested in spreading their religion, Catholicism, throughout the world.

Europeans consider their search for new land and wealth

CHAPTER 2
Ships Sail

People in London, England, during the late 1500s found themselves in very close quarters. London was extremely crowded. Bubonic plague, smallpox, tuberculosis, and malaria regularly broke out. The water was not clean enough to drink. Diseases that come from dirty water, like cholera, were common. London was also expensive. And landlords charged high rents. Outside the city, farmland was hard to own if you were young or poor.

Queen Elizabeth I ruled over this busy, crowded place and all of England and Ireland. She knew about the scarce farmland, cramped houses, and dirty water, but she had other worries on her mind, too. Spain was building a whole new fleet of warships that they could use to attack English ships.

Queen Elizabeth I

Elizabeth's powerful adviser Sir Walter Raleigh told her that if England could make a permanent settlement in the new land of North America, they could use it as a base to attack

Spanish ships. England could then have the land and any valuable resources they found there, too.

Raleigh decided that some ships should sail to the coast of what is now the Carolinas to explore the land and find the best place for a colony. In April 1584, almost forty years before the *Mayflower* would reach what we now call New England, two ships, commanded by Philip Amadas and Arthur Barlowe, set sail from England. On July 13, they landed on the barrier islands that are now called the Outer Banks.

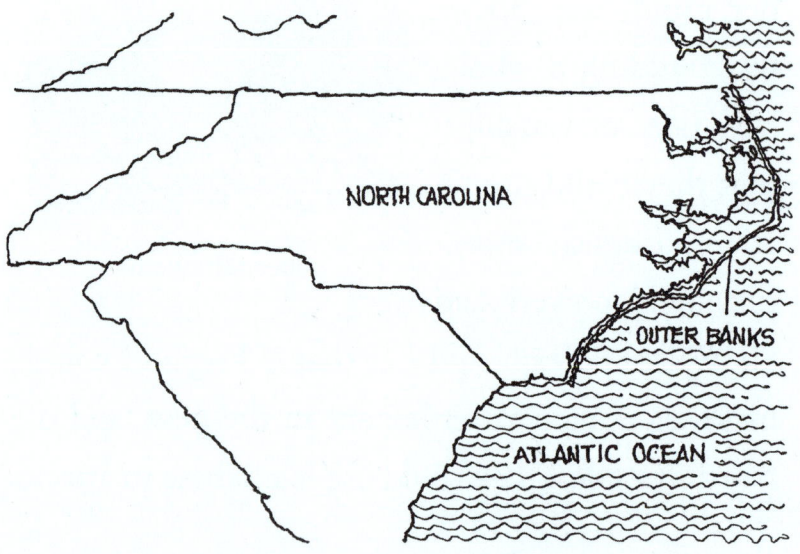

When Amadas and Barlowe saw what is
now Roanoke Island, about twelve miles long
and three miles wide, they thought they had
found the perfect spot. They noted that the
soil was wholesome, sweet, and good for crops.
A group of people, who might have been Secotan
or Roanoke, welcomed them. The tribal leader,
Wingina, was recuperating from a thigh wound
in a distant town, but his brother, Granganimeo,
offered to trade with the Europeans.

Sir Walter Raleigh (c. 1553–1618)

Sir Walter Raleigh was born in the English countryside and served in the army as a young man. Handsome and charming, he was a favorite of Queen Elizabeth I. Raleigh organized and raised money for three expeditions to North America, in 1584, 1585, and 1587. Raleigh himself did not travel to North America, but he did sail twice to South America to explore there.

The queen wanted Raleigh to be loyal only to her, and when he secretly married her lady-in-waiting Bess Throckmorton, she was angry. She had the couple locked in the Tower of London, a royal fortress, palace, and prison. The Raleighs were released after a few months, but Sir Walter was banned from the queen's court.

After the queen died in 1603, the new king, James I, suspected Raleigh of plotting against him. He again imprisoned Raleigh in the Tower of London, this time for thirteen years. When Raleigh was released, he went on one last expedition to South America, in 1616. During the trip, his men attacked a Spanish settlement. King James had Raleigh arrested for stirring up trouble and sentenced him to death. He was beheaded on October 29, 1618.

Over the next few days, the Indigenous people offered deer skins, pearls, and dyes in exchange for tin dishes, knives, and axes. As the Europeans grew more comfortable, Barlowe took seven men on an exploring expedition in their smaller boat. They visited Granganimeo's village, on the same island, where they were welcomed by Granganimeo's wife.

The Europeans were dirty and smelly after both their long journey across the ocean and their shorter journey to the village. Granganimeo's wife, whose name is not known, invited them into her house and washed some of their clothes. Other women washed Amadas's and Barlowe's feet and cooked them a meal of venison, roast fish, fruit, corn pudding, and wine with ginger and sassafras.

The men were given leftovers and reed mats to use as umbrellas when they returned to their boat to sleep. Granganimeo and his wife had a reason to treat the captains so well. They might have been hoping that making friends with the Europeans would help them politically. They would have formed a partnership with the outsiders that some of the other Algonquian nations would not.

Amadas and Barlowe decided that they would tell everyone back in England that the coastal Carolinas were a perfect place for settlement. But they had barely explored. They could see that the Algonquian people grew good crops, but they did not know what farming techniques they used. They wanted their trip to be a success. So they decided to report that it had been, even without knowing many details about the land they had visited. And they had only visited a single island.

Two members of allied Algonquian groups—
Wanchese, who was a part of the Roanoke
Nation living on or near Roanoke Island, and
Manteo, who was Croatoan
and whose people lived
on Croatoan Island—
traveled to England
with the explorers
when they left for
home. We're not
certain why, but
they may have been
sent by their leaders
who believed that
making friends with
the English would be helpful to their people.

In England, Sir Walter Raleigh was delighted
to hear the two captains' report about the coastal
Carolinas. Raleigh brought Wanchese and Manteo
to visit Parliament, the seat of government.

Wanchese

Parliament, 1584

Their homeland was rich and bountiful, they declared to the elected officials. Raleigh wanted to lobby the members of the British government for enough money to establish a full colony.

Manteo

Manteo was a leader and member of the Croatoan Nation of Algonquian people and was a friend to the colonial settlers for as long as there is a record of him. He sailed to England on two separate journeys, in 1584 and 1586. There, he wore English clothes made of brown taffeta and stayed at a home of Sir Walter Raleigh. Eventually, Manteo learned English and taught the Algonquian language to others who were interested in learning about Algonquian life.

On Roanoke Island, Manteo helped the English colonists by interpreting for them with different Algonquian groups. He also tried to convince Croatoans and others not to fight the English. He was baptized and became a member of the Church of England in August 1587. Manteo is the first Native person to be baptized into the Church of England.

And Raleigh got what he wanted. On April 9, 1585, under the command of Sir Richard Grenville, five big ships and two small ones left England for the Carolina coast, with about six hundred men aboard—and only men. No women and children were included. Their plan was to establish a permanent English colony.

Sir Richard Grenville

About half the men were professional sailors and many in the other half were soldiers and craftsmen, such as carpenters, smiths, and cooks. Others were gentlemen and friends, relatives, and neighbors of Sir Walter Raleigh. Some were laborers and regular citizens.

Overall, Raleigh modeled this trip after a military expedition and chose men who could fight, live in rough conditions, and obey orders. They carried weapons, supplies, and mining and scientific equipment. Ralph Lane, a professional soldier, would become the governor of this new settlement. Manteo and Wanchese were also aboard. They had been away from their home for eight months.

The expedition arrived in the Outer Banks in June 1585, about three months after leaving England. Everyone got off the boats and made a new plan. The food supplies were low, and there wasn't enough left to feed everyone. Sir Grenville and Ralph Lane decided that Lane and about one hundred men would stay on

Roanoke Island over the winter. But they could not stay there permanently. The water around the island was too shallow for big English ships to anchor. Instead, the larger sailing ships had to anchor several miles offshore.

Lane and his men would make Roanoke Island their base and use their smaller boats to scout the mainland for a more suitable permanent site for the colony. Meanwhile, Grenville and the others would go back to England and get supplies.

They would return in the spring, around Easter. The leader Wingina offered land to those staying on Roanoke Island, and Lane's  men immediately got started on a fort and houses to live in. They needed the fort to protect themselves in case the Spanish found the English settlement and decided to attack.

Spanish colonial flag

Soon after they landed, Wanchese returned to his own people on Roanoke Island. Manteo tried to meet with him, but Wanchese refused to have anything more to do with the English, who now had lost a valuable ally.

While on a visit to a Secotan village called Aquascogoc, the English could not find one of their silver drinking cups. They accused the villagers of stealing it and demanded it back.

When they did not receive it back, they burned the village houses and corn crops to the ground in a shocking act of violence. The English did not write down why they did this, just that they did. This extreme overreaction may have been meant to teach the Secotan a lesson about disobeying the English, even though the English were not their rulers. The Secotan people were furious. How dare the English burn their homes and farmland?

At this time, some of the Native people on Roanoke Island started to get sick. The men who had arrived from England were spreading germs that the villagers had never been exposed to and couldn't protect themselves from. Many Native people began to see the English as dangerous and harmful.

The Algonquian began to wish that their visitors would go home. They had shared food with them. They had even made fish traps for them. But now it was time for them to leave. By early March 1586, the English settlers began to run out of food. They asked the Secotan people to give them corn. But the Secotan did not have enough for a hundred extra people and eventually refused. Easter, the time for Grenville to return, came and went with no sign of the resupply ships.

Then, Wingina made a decision: If the English wouldn't leave, he would fight. He gathered other groups together and made plans to attack. But the English had an advantage. They had captured an Algonquian prisoner, and he warned them of the coming fight.

The English decided to strike first. They tried to steal tribal-owned canoes, and violence broke out. The English beheaded some Native people the next morning. They landed canoes near Wingina's village.

They fired on it with their pistols. Wingina headed for the woods. The English ran after him and killed him.

The Algonquian people were not going to witness the murder of their leader and do nothing. Ralph Lane knew that. But he still wanted to look for a permanent colony site and wait for Grenville and his supplies.

Then, in early June 1586, a fleet of ships appeared off the coast. They were commanded by the famous explorer Sir Francis Drake, who had been on a monthslong expedition around the West Indies and the Florida coast. Part of his mission, which Lane did not know about, was to check on the colony.

Sir Francis Drake (c. 1540–1596)

Sir Francis Drake was the son of tenant farmers in Devonshire, England, and first went to sea when he was about eighteen. In the 1560s, he began commanding his own ships as well and led English slave-trading expeditions to the West Indies, pirating expeditions against Spanish ports in the

Caribbean, and, in 1577, an expedition around South America to the Pacific Ocean. Drake continued west to the Philippines, eventually reaching England again. He was the first English person to sail around the world.

Drake was celebrated and knighted by Queen Elizabeth I. In 1587, he served as the second-in-command in the English victory over the Spanish Armada. Drake died of dysentery in 1596 off the coast of what is now Panama, and his body was buried at sea.

Lane and his men were very glad to see Drake. He offered them supplies, sailors, and ships so that they could keep looking for their colony site. Lane gratefully agreed. But as the men were talking and making plans, on June 13, a hurricane blew up.

It destroyed several of Drake's large and small boats, along with the supplies that were onboard, and it snapped the anchor cables on others, so that they drifted out to sea.

Lane had had enough. He abruptly changed his mind and decided that he and his men would leave with the English fleet. Drake agreed, and at the last minute, Manteo decided to come along as well. In late June, Drake's remaining ships pulled up their anchors. The wind caught at their sails, and the big ships glided away from the Carolina coast. The colony was abandoned. It had failed.

In late August, Grenville returned to Roanoke Island from England, not knowing that Lane and his men had left. He brought ships, supplies, and men. But when he found the abandoned buildings, he decided not to stay. Instead, he dropped off fifteen men with some weapons to guard the buildings. Then he, too, left, and sailed back to England.

CHAPTER 3
A Permanent Colony

Ralph Lane was back in England and had reported to Sir Walter Raleigh that their year had been full of Algonquian attacks and starvation. They had needed resupply, and Grenville's ships did not arrive in time. But should they try again? This was the question Sir Walter Raleigh was pondering.

Lane said that land on Roanoke Island was not fertile enough to produce the necessary quantities of crops to support a permanent colony. But a future expedition could perhaps establish a colony on the mainland, inland from the Outer Banks. Raleigh listened. He and other wealthy men had already invested a lot of money into these trips, and they hoped a colony could succeed. They would try one more time.

This time, the colony would be set up differently. Now John White, an artist who

John White

had been on the 1585 expedition with Barlowe and Amadas, would be governor. White was not a soldier like Ralph Lane, so this trip would not be set up like a military expedition. Instead, the settlement was meant to feel more like an English village. John White wanted to establish a more democratic set of rules for the colony. This journey would have women and children along, too.

They would try to set up a permanent colony— and they would not stay on Roanoke Island. They would pause there, to rest, before moving on to a better site on the mainland. There, they would farm and grow their own food. Eventually, they would make their own clothes and raise crops to send back to England. They would establish trade with the Algonquian, exchanging beads, cloth, and copper for deerskins and sassafras to send back to England as well.

Sassafras

The journey was announced. Eventually, 120 people agreed to sail (115 of whom intended to remain on Roanoke Island). They were mainly ordinary citizens—lawyers, shopkeepers, and farmers. One was a sheriff. One was a mother nursing her baby and two were pregnant women. John White's daughter, Eleanor Dare, was one of the pregnant women. They were hoping for land of their own and a chance to grow their wealth by farming, exploring, and trading. Nine children went along, alone or with their parents. Manteo

also joined the colonists so that he could travel home.

On May 8, 1587, a fleet of three boats raised their sails and set out from Plymouth, England, into the Atlantic Ocean's choppy waters, bound for Roanoke Island. The *Lion* was the flagship and carried most of the passengers.

The *Lion*

Hardtack

A cargo ship followed, and a smaller boat called a pinnace bobbed alongside.

The food they had packed included a kind of very tough biscuit called hardtack, cheese, beer, oatmeal, butter, and various salted meats—beef, pork, and fish. They brought blankets, clothes, tools for farming, pots, pans, armor, guns, and spears. They also brought glass beads and copper to trade with the Algonquian.

More than two months after leaving England, the faint outline of the Outer Banks appeared. And on July 22, the *Lion* dropped its anchor in the deep water. They had made it to Roanoke!

CHAPTER 4
The Struggle on Roanoke

Everyone knew that Roanoke Island was to be only a temporary stop. There, they would have the chance to rest, hunt, and gather themselves for the trip to the inland site that would be their permanent home, fifty miles into the mainland.

And the colonists didn't have much time. In just five months, it would be winter. They were supposed to check on the fifteen men who had stayed behind from Grenville's group, then move on. The men, women, and children climbed into the small pinnace that would ferry them to the shore of Roanoke Island. But then, their world shifted.

The pilot of the expedition, Simon Fernandes, did not want to sail farther inland. He was hoping to sail to the West Indies—a name that at this time referred to the group of Caribbean islands off the coast of Florida that today includes places such as Cuba, Haiti, Jamaica, and Puerto Rico—to steal treasure from Spanish ships. Fernandes wanted to take this journey after the return trip to England.

Pinnace

And it was already late in the season. He didn't want to waste more time. Fernandes shouted to the sailors on the pinnace that they should leave their passengers on the island and then anchor with him offshore to rest for a few weeks on the bigger ships. No one but John White and a couple of others would be allowed back on the ships.

We don't know why John White didn't protest. Perhaps he thought other English ships would come along soon to help them. The sailors left the settlers on Roanoke Island. Then they rowed back to the ships and stayed there, bobbing far offshore from the island.

The English settlers were scared. They had been abandoned in the place where Lane's men had murdered Wingina. They worried that the Native people would want revenge. None of the men Sir Richard Grenville had left on the island were still there. All that the newcomers found in their little encampment was one human skeleton. Everyone else had vanished.

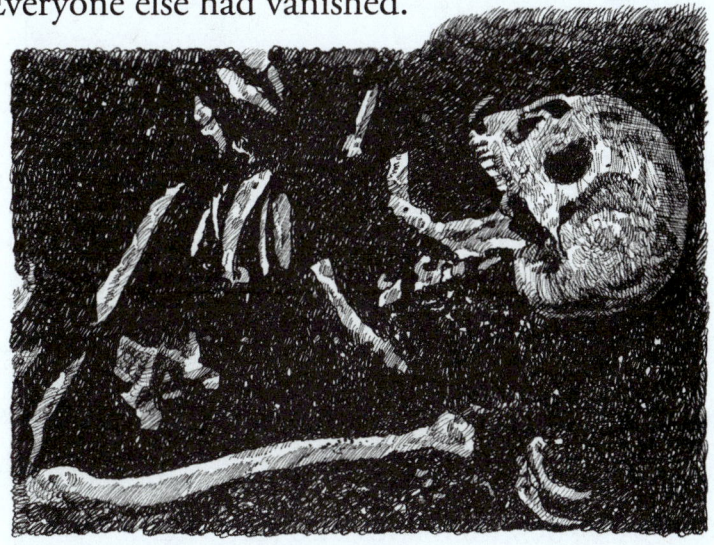

Forced to stay on Roanoke Island through the winter, they began dragging their supplies to one end of the island, where Lane's fort had been.

They found melons and squash that Lane's men had planted. Then they got busy unpacking and setting up their homes. John had even brought paintings and books from home. Perhaps they could live together with the Algonquian peoples, John likely thought. The violence and murder done by Lane's men could be forgotten.

Six days after they arrived, a man named George Howe went for a walk. When he was about two miles from the fort, George decided to catch some crabs in the shallow, warm water near the shore. He undressed and waded in with a spear. It was summer, and the weather was warm.

But George wasn't alone. A group of Roanoke were watching him from the trees near the shore. They sprang at George and shot him with sixteen arrows, then beat him with wooden clubs. His body was left floating in the water.

George was killed in revenge for Wingina's murder. The English colony was shaken by the news. John decided to send a group of his friends to talk to Manteo and his fellow Croatoans. He assumed they would tell the British men anything they knew.

But the meeting didn't go exactly as planned.

The Croatoans felt threatened when the Europeans approached and tried to shoot them with arrows. Manteo rushed out and called to both groups in their own languages, telling them to put down their weapons.

John's friends asked for food, and the Croatoans fed them, even though they themselves barely had enough food to spare. They showed the Europeans one of their own men, who was paralyzed. This man had been hit by an English bullet during the fight that had killed Wingina.

The Croatoans may have been friendly toward the group of British men that day, but they also had not forgotten the past. As for the fifteen men Grenville had left behind, the Croatoans said, Wingina's people had killed them all. One of the leaders of this attack was Wanchese, the Roanoke who had traveled to England with Manteo. Now Wanchese was leading attacks on the English. The Croatoans would try to reason with Wanchese's people, they said. They asked to be given one week's time.

John's group went back to their settlement. They waited. A week passed with no word from the Croatoans. On August 9, a group of Englishmen— and Manteo—decided to attack first. They crept toward what they thought was Wanchese's village.

A fire was burning, and people were scattered around it. Someone gave a signal, and the English charged, shooting and hitting one man. Only then did they realize that they were attacking Croatoans, not Wanchese's people—they were hurting their friends and allies.

Wanchese and his people had already left the area, the Europeans found out later. The Croatoans were looking for any items they might have left behind. If the Europeans had just waited patiently, the Croatoans said, they would have reported back, as they'd promised. Now the Europeans had killed some of their friends, and they still hadn't made peace with their enemies.

Back in the settlement, there was good news, though. On August 18, 1587, John's daughter, Eleanor, gave birth to a daughter named Virginia.

She was the first child born in the settlement and the first European child born in the colony.

But winter was barreling toward the settlement,

and the fleet anchored offshore was getting ready to leave. Everyone on Roanoke Island needed supplies and bigger ships in order to get to Chesapeake Bay, where they hoped to settle permanently. Together, the group decided that John White should sail back to England with the fleet. There, he'd ask for more money from Sir Walter Raleigh so that he could buy supplies. He would come back as soon as he could. The group all agreed that this was the best solution.

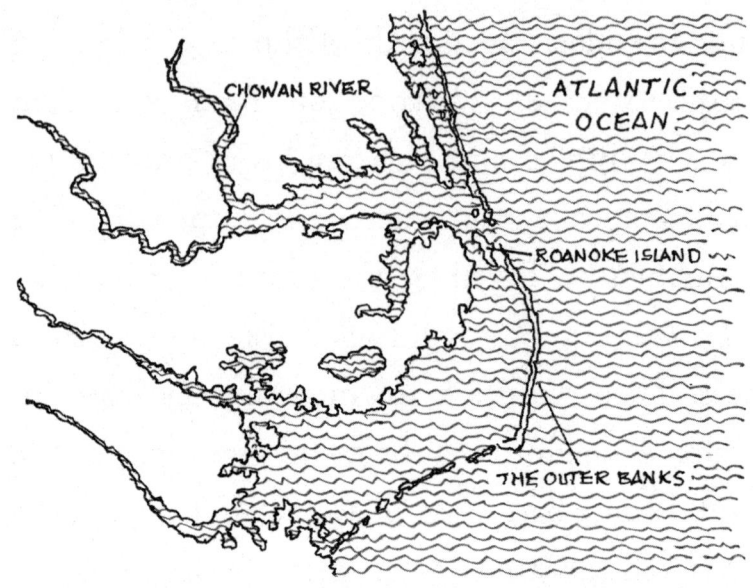

John agreed to go. But the Europeans didn't want to stay on Roanoke Island—they had never meant to. While John was gone, they would use the pinnace to travel about fifty miles inland and to the west, where they might find more food and friendly people to help them. This would put them near the mouth of a river now called the Chowan. But they would leave behind a small group on Roanoke, so they could tell John where the others had gone. They worked out a code: If the group left behind on Roanoke also had to leave, they would carve the name of the place they had gone to on a tree, so John could find them. If they had been attacked or were leaving in distress, they would carve a cross over the name.

The group promised to take care of the pictures and books that John had brought from England and was leaving behind. John said goodbye to his family, including baby Virginia, who was less than two weeks old. He boarded the ship that would carry him back to England. On August 27, the crew pulled up the giant anchors, and they glided away from shore.

CHAPTER 5
John Finally Returns

John White was aboard the ship for over two months. His return trip was plagued with problems. The ship ran into a terrible storm near the coast of Ireland, which pushed the vessel back out into the open ocean. By the time the crew managed to wrestle the ship back to the Irish coast, they had been delayed so long that they were out of food. Nearly a third of the crew had died, either on the journey from Roanoke Island or soon after the ship reached Ireland. John finally reached England on November 8, 1587.

Soon after arriving in England, John went to see Sir Walter Raleigh. He had to get money for more ships and more supplies for the colony as soon as possible. Raleigh agreed to send a small ship quickly, packed with supplies. That ship would also carry the news that a larger fleet of ships would arrive by the following summer.

But these ships never sailed. Queen Elizabeth I was preparing to defend her country against Spain, which was soon to launch its navy, the Spanish Armada. At last, in the spring of 1588, the resupply ships Raleigh had ordered were ready to sail to

Roanoke Island. But before they could set out, the queen declared that no ship could leave England without her permission. She wanted all ships to stay in England in case they were needed to defend the coast against the armada.

The Spanish Armada, 1588

England fought the Spanish Armada and defeated it in the summer of 1588. The rule against ships leaving was finally lifted. But by then, Sir Walter Raleigh was busy with other projects.

Queen Elizabeth wanted to colonize Ireland and had given Raleigh land there, with orders to settle English families on it. The colony at Roanoke was low on Raleigh's list of priorities.

John White was not giving up on sending resupply ships back to the colony, though. In March 1590, almost three years after leaving Roanoke Island, John managed to arrange for two ships, the *Hopewell* and the *Moonlight*, to carry him and supplies to Roanoke on their way to the West Indies. On March 20, the *Hopewell* and the *Moonlight* left England, sailing to the Canary Islands, off the coast of Spain, then on to the Caribbean, finally sailing for Roanoke at the end of July.

On the evening of August 15, the *Hopewell* anchored close enough to Roanoke Island to see land and the fire burning there. John wrote later that he had hoped that meant some of the colonists were there, waiting. On August 17,

John and two boatloads of sailors, including both captains, rowed toward Roanoke Island, fighting the ferocious waves, with the supplies getting soaked. One boat turned over and the captain of the *Moonlight*, its first mate, the ship's surgeon, and four other sailors drowned.

The next day, on shore, they studied the tree into which *CRO* was carved. This was the sign that the villagers had said they would leave if they decided to abandon the village, and there was no cross over the letters, meaning the villagers had not been attacked.

In the village, on a fence post, they found the carved word *CROATOAN*—again with no cross above it. This meant that for reasons John and the sailors did not know, the villagers had probably gone safely to their friends, the Croatoans, Manteo's people, who lived on Croatoan Island to the south. The main group of villagers may have gone on to the site fifty miles into the mainland, but they did not leave a message.

John and his crew went back to their boat and rowed out to the big ships. A storm was blowing in, so they made a plan to spend the night on the ships, then move to Croatoan Island in the morning.

But that night, in the storm, the *Hopewell* lost three of its four anchors, and was driven by the wind farther out into open water. The sailors were already worried about their food and freshwater supplies, and now they had only one anchor. The captain of the *Hopewell* decided they should not waste more time sailing to Croatoan Island. Instead, the *Hopewell* would head to the Caribbean to spend the winter. They'd return to Roanoke Island in the spring. Meanwhile, the *Moonlight* would sail straight back to England.

Although he was so close to Croatoan Island and his family, John agreed to this plan. He didn't have much choice. The captain had already decided, and the crew agreed.

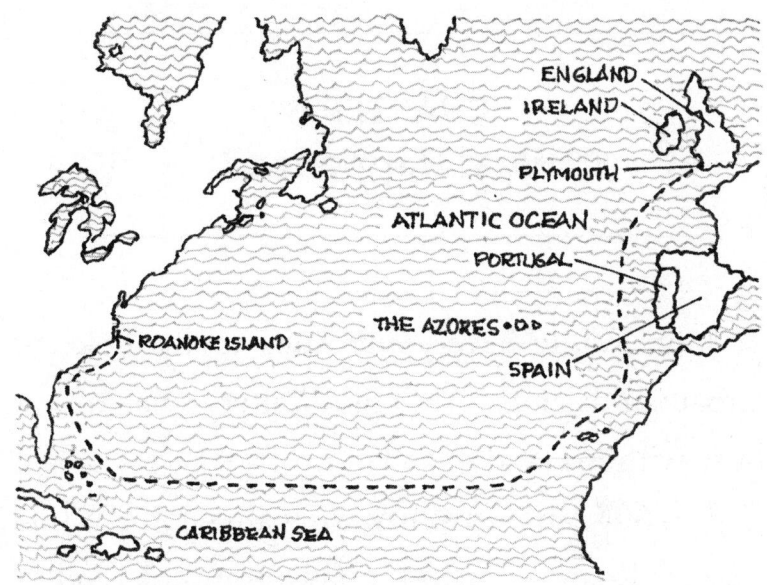

The *Hopewell* sailed out into the open sea and set a course south for the Caribbean. But when strong winds pushed the ship toward the east, the captain gave up the plan to go to the Caribbean. Instead, the *Hopewell* followed the wind to the Azores, off the coast of Portugal. Then the ship sailed on to England, landing at Plymouth on October 24, 1590. John White was still aboard. But his hopes of seeing the lost colonists again had been left far behind.

CHAPTER 6
What Happened?

John White never went back to Roanoke or Croatoan Islands. And Sir Walter Raleigh was busy with his land in Ireland.

In 1607, about twenty years after John White last left Roanoke Island, a new group of English colonists arrived in North America. These 144 men and boys had been sent to try once again to make a new colony work. Their investors, the Virginia Company, were convinced that if they settled farther to the north, they could be successful along the Virginia and North Carolina coasts.

This time, the Europeans picked a village site near Chesapeake Bay, one hundred miles northwest of Roanoke Island. They named their new village Jamestown, and soon after they arrived, they tried to find the Roanoke colonists. John Smith, the leader of the colony, twice sent expeditions to the area around Roanoke Island to search.

John Smith

Around 1609, the secretary of the Jamestown colony, William Strachey, spoke with two Native men, who were named Namontack and Machumps. Machumps told Strachey that the Roanoke colonists had made their way to an area near Chesapeake Bay. They lived there for about twenty years and became friendly with the Chesapeake people. But then, around the time that the Jamestown settlers arrived, the colonists were killed by a leader named Powhatan (whose given name

was Wahunsonacock) and his confederacy. The Chesapeake band had refused to join Powhatan's confederacy, and the colonists were living alongside them at the time. So Powhatan ordered both the Chesapeake band and the Europeans

Powhatan

killed together. Machumps said that seven Europeans had escaped and were living with a leader named Eyanoco, but the Jamestown colonists never found them.

One hundred years later, in 1709, rumors about Roanoke swirled again. An English explorer named John Lawson wrote that he had visited with a group of Croatoan, and that several people in this group had gray eyes. These

John Lawson

Croatoan people told Lawson that their ancestors were Europeans and that they could "talk in a book"—meaning that they could read English.

These could have been the descendants of the Roanoke colonists who had carved *CRO* on the tree. If this is true, then that group of the English villagers lived peacefully with the Croatoan for a hundred years, marrying among them and having children.

The trail of Roanoke became folded into the story of the European colonization of North America. As the centuries went on, more clues started to emerge—this time not from stories, but from actual objects on Roanoke Island.

The Virginia Company

The Virginia Company was created by English merchants in 1606, with the mission of founding a colony along the east coast of North America.  Wealthy Londoners could buy parts of the company, called shares, and when the company made money, they would get a portion of its profits.

The Virginia Company was given a charter—or royal permission to exist—by King James I. After the failure of the Jamestown settlement, King James took the charter back in 1624. The Virginia Company was disbanded, and the land around Jamestown, Virginia, became a royal colony of England.

CHAPTER 7
Exploring the Artifacts

In 2012, Dr. Brent Lane was looking at an old map. Dr. Lane was a professor of heritage economics at the University of North Carolina at Chapel Hill. Part of his job was to study the way people in the past lived. In this case, he was looking at a map that John White had drawn.

The map was in the British Museum in London, and Dr. Lane was trying to find the location of a certain Secotan village. John had marked various features on the map: rivers, the outline of the coast, the location of the Roanoke

Dr. Brent Lane

colony. But Dr. Lane saw something else, too—a patch. A little piece of blank paper had been cut out and glued onto the map. Could it be hiding something?

Dr. Lane knew that sometimes old mapmakers like John White would use patches to correct mistakes or to cover up things. So he asked the museum's technicians to look under the small paper patch with X-rays and other imaging technology.

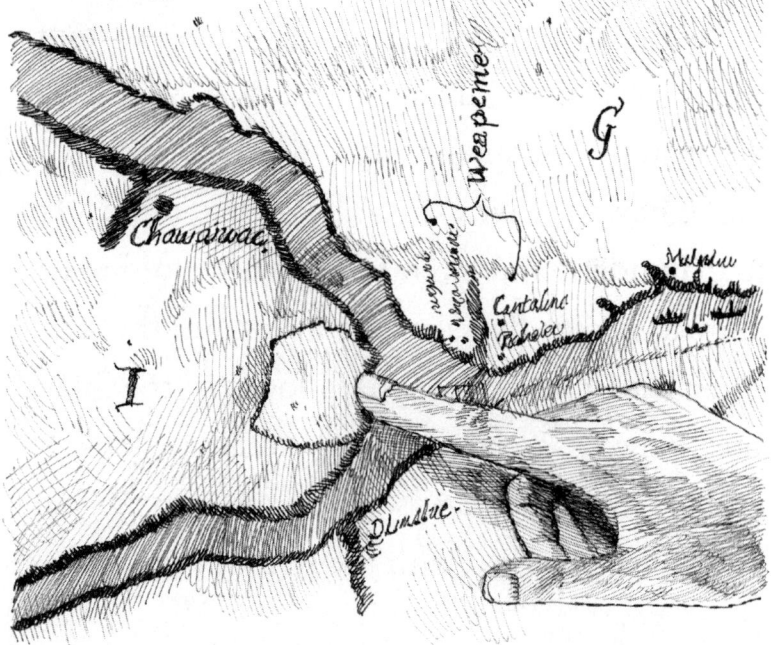

 When they did, they found a blue and red star had been drawn on the map. It was the type of mark that would note a fort or a settlement. John had drawn the star, but then he had covered it up. He had probably done this so that if Spanish spies found the map, they wouldn't know where the settlement was.

Before John White left Roanoke Island, the villagers had told him they were going to move about fifty miles inland—and that was where this patch was on the map, near the mouth of the Chowan River, in Albemarle Sound. For four hundred and twenty-five years, no one had known about the star markings on the map. They hadn't known where to look for the inland site. Now, if archaeologists wanted to look for artifacts of the villagers, they could try digging at the place marked with the star on the map!

John White's map, 1585–1586

Archaeologists found pieces of pottery that they knew English people used around the time of the Roanoke colony. And they found little pieces of metal that European people used to stretch animal hides and fasten pieces of wool cloth. Archaeologists already knew that these bits of metal were also from the time of the Roanoke colony.

But there was a problem: All these artifacts were made or brought by Europeans and from the time of Roanoke, but the dating technology that the archaeologists use can only tell how old artifacts are within a range of a few decades. So the objects might have been from a later decade. Algonquian groups could have traded for these artifacts somewhere else as well, and used them in their own villages, which were in the area.

If the archaeologists could find a grave with human bones or a piece of writing with a date, they could be sure that they had identified the spot where the villagers had settled. But some believed that proof had already been found, almost eighty years before, on the banks of a North Carolina river.

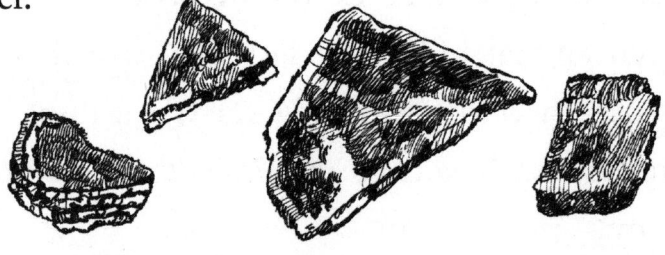

Fragments of British pottery

CHAPTER 8
The Chowan River Stone

Chowan River swamp

Louis Hammond just wanted to find some hickory nuts. In 1937, the California man was nut-hunting in a swamp close to the Chowan River, near the North Carolina border with Virginia. He was about sixty-five miles west of

Roanoke Island. But Louis found something more than nuts: a large gray stone, weighing about twenty-one pounds, sticking out of the ground. It was covered with white markings like letters.

Hammond didn't know it then, but he was near the inland spot John White had marked with a star on his map.

Hammond took the stone to Emory University in Atlanta. And there, professors told him that the markings *were* letters. Louis had found what looked like a note written on the rock by

Eleanor Dare, John White's daughter and the mother of Virginia, the first European baby born in North America.

The note said that after John left, the villagers went inland as they had planned. They suffered from misery and war, as the writer put it, for two years. They got sick, too, until only twenty-four of them were left. They were attacked, in 1591, and everyone was killed except for seven people. The dead had been buried four miles up a river, the writer said, and their names were marked on a rock. On the other side, the writer wrote her initials: EWD—Eleanor White Dare.

This is the same number of survivors that Machumps had described to William Strachey, but this attack takes place in 1591, soon after John White left for England, and apparently near the mouth of the Chowan River. The attack Machumps described would have taken place in 1607, much later, and somewhere on the south side of Chesapeake Bay, a hundred miles or more away from the mouth of the Chowan. The Chowan River Stone (also known as the Dare Stone) described a new possible fate of the lost colonists.

The professors at Emory University declared that the stone was the real thing—it was authentic. Hammond had left Atlanta, but when the university wanted to ask him more questions, Hammond was nowhere to be found.

The professors at Emory had said the stone was real, but now they were suspicious. Coincidentally, 1937 was also the 350th anniversary of the birth of Virginia Dare. The nation was paying a lot of attention to the Roanoke anniversary. President Franklin D. Roosevelt had even recently visited the area to highlight the anniversary. Maybe Hammond had faked the stone to get famous or cash in on some of the interest in Roanoke.

In 2016, geologists from the University of North Carolina at Asheville cut a slab from the bottom of the stone. They examined the inside of the stone compared to the outside. The inside was a lot brighter than the dark carvings on the outside. This told the geologists that the carvings could have been very old.

If the Chowan River Stone was a fake, the carvings would have been brighter and not as weathered, since they would have been carved only about eighty years ago, instead of four hundred and twenty-five. This could mean the stone was real.

On the other hand, some of the words on the stone were not the types of words someone in Eleanor Dare's time would have used. She also signed her name with initials, EWD. This was not the usual way women signed their names in the late 1500s. Scientists still do not agree on whether these clues prove that the Chowan River Stone is a fake. Instead of providing answers to the fate of the lost colonists, the Chowan River Stone only offered another possible ending to their story.

CHAPTER 9
The Story Continues

The smaller group of colonists who carved *CRO* and *CROATOAN* on the tree and the fence post might have had a different ending. They may have lived peacefully for many years, stayed healthy, married Native husbands and wives, and had children.

Today, Croatoan Island is called Hatteras Island, about fifty miles south of Roanoke Island. There, archaeologists have dug up a mix of English and Indigenous artifacts. Parts of guns, shards of glass, and writing slates are mixed in with local Native pottery.

Writing slate found on Hatteras Island

They found part of a sword, too. These were very special personal items, the kind people kept with them throughout their lives, in the places where they lived. Europeans probably wouldn't have traded them to other groups.

The British settlers might have built homes in their own style among the Croatoan homes, too. They used square posts for building, and the Croatoans used round posts. Archaeologists have uncovered both square and round post holes mixed in together, as if the two groups were living side by side as neighbors.

Like the Chowan River Stone and the artifacts dug up near the mouth of the Chowan River, these are strong clues, but they are *only* clues. Because archaeologists didn't find a piece of writing with a date or human bones that could be dated with technology here, either, they weren't able to say for sure what happened to the colonists. They couldn't rule out that the sword and the other artifacts were not, in fact, traded by the colonists to groups that carried them to other regions.

Remains of a British sword found on Hatteras Island

For hundreds of years, the story of Roanoke was folded into the general history of the United

States. But in 1834, a historian named George Bancroft published a book called *A History of the United States, from the Discovery of the American Continent to the Present Time*, and in it he declared that Virginia Dare was a symbol of the beginnings of a new nation. Soon, other people began to make a hero out of Virginia Dare. Because she was the first white European baby born in the United States, people wanted to celebrate her. At a time when racism toward Black and brown people was pervasive and unchecked, telling this story about Virginia Dare—and Roanoke— was a way of declaring that white people were in control of the country and had been for a very long time.

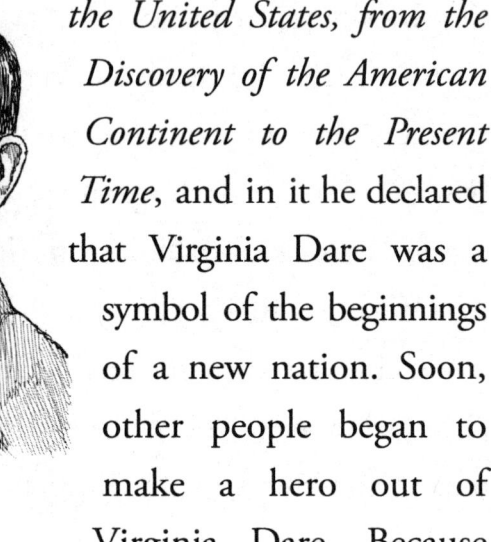

George Bancroft

The writer Sallie Southall Cotten encouraged this racist legend with a long poem called *The White Doe*, published in 1901. The poem describes Virginia turning into a beautiful white deer and then being wounded by Native people. Later, suffragists working for women's right to vote used Virginia's name on leaflets to try to convince lawmakers to give the vote to women before Black people. Her name was even used to advertise products, as a symbol of someone white and pure.

And Roanoke continued to keep its grip on people's imaginations. In 1921, the silent film *Lost Colony* flickered on movie screens, and just sixteen years later, in 1937, the play *The Lost Colony* opened on Roanoke Island. It is still being performed today. People can even visit the Roanoke colony in person today—or at least an imagining of that world—at the Roanoke Island Festival Park, where costumed interpreters try to

Elizabeth Grimball directing *Lost Colony*, 1921

show visitors what life on Roanoke in the late 1500s was like.

The "lost" colony still inspires people today and is often featured in TV shows and books. Without knowing for sure what happened at Roanoke, people have made up—and continue to make up—their own stories about it. But the story of Roanoke is most likely one about people living side by side.

Freedmen's Colony

There was another, not lost colony on Roanoke: the Freedmen's Colony. It was founded by the Union Army during the Civil War, after the victory at the Battle of Roanoke Island, as a settlement community for Black people, some of whom were formerly enslaved. It functioned as a "safe haven."

The Freedmen's Colony existed from 1862 to 1867, when it was decommissioned. Most of the residents settled elsewhere on the mainland at that time, but descendants of the Freedmen's Colony still live on Roanoke Island today.

FIRST LIGHT OF FREEDOM

Monument honoring the Freedmen's Colony

The Lumbee people, who have lived in the Carolinas for hundreds of years, have said that their ancestors probably knew the Roanoke villagers, married them, and lived with them. Over the decades and centuries, many people came to the coastal Carolinas—Europeans,

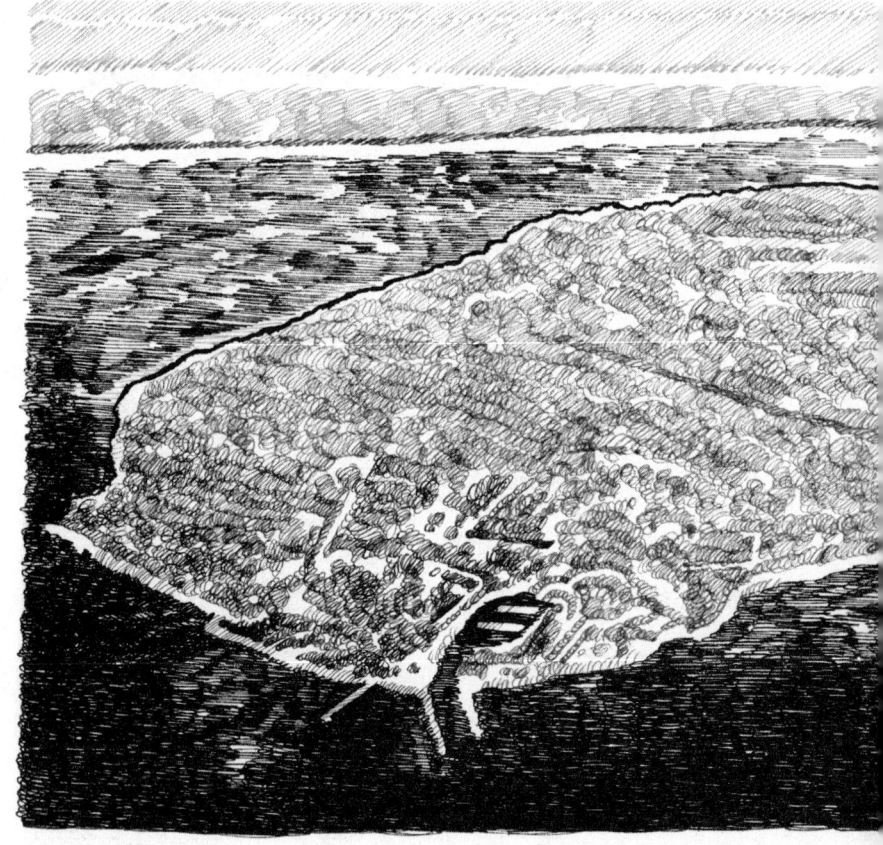

enslaved people, and other Indigenous groups. These people sometimes fought brutally, sometimes married and had families together. Their history continues to this day, and perhaps the residents of the lost colony of Roanoke are still a part of it.

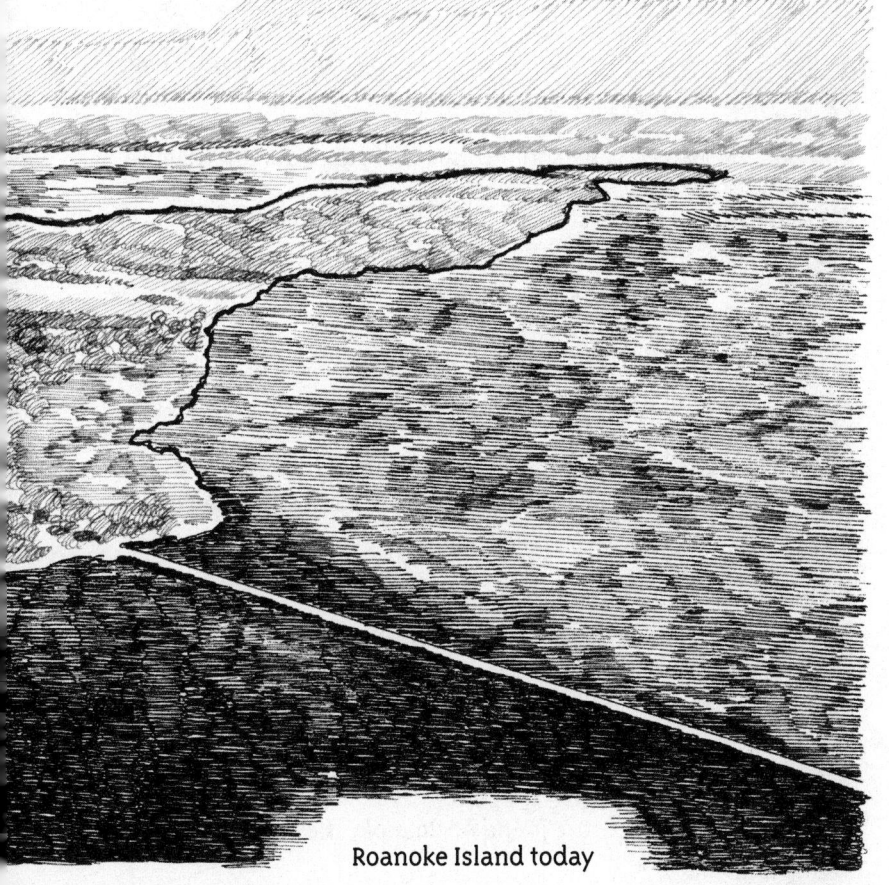

Roanoke Island today

Timeline of the Lost Colony of Roanoke

2500–2000 BC	Indigenous people first move to the Outer Banks coastal islands of what is now North Carolina
AD 700	The Algonquian people are living in the coastal region of what is now North Carolina
1584	First English expedition to Roanoke Island arrives
1585	Second English expedition to Roanoke Island arrives, led by Sir Richard Grenville
1586	Ralph Lane and the other men abandon the colony
	Richard Grenville returns and leaves fifteen men
1587	John White and the other colonists arrive on Roanoke Island on July 22
	Virginia Dare is born on August 18
	White leaves for England on August 27
1590	John White returns to Roanoke Island, finds the colony abandoned, and finds messages carved into a tree and a fence post
1937	Louis Hammond finds the Chowan River Stone in a swamp near the North Carolina–Virginia border
2012	Star marking a fort is found on John White's map by Professor Brent Lane
2023	Algonquian peoples' artifacts mixed with European artifacts are found on Roanoke Island

Timeline of the World

15,000 BC	Villagers in what is now Central America farm pumpkins, chiles, and beans
3400 BC	Writing is developed in Sumer, Mesopotamia, near what is now Iraq
31 BC	Roman Empire is founded
AD 1534	King Henry VIII founds the Church of England
1610	Galileo observes that the Earth and other planets revolve around the Sun
1620	The Pilgrims arrive from England on the *Mayflower* to what is now Plymouth, Massachusetts
1644	The Ming dynasty ends in China
1861	The American Civil War begins
1906	A massive earthquake hits San Francisco, California, killing more than three thousand people and, with the fire that followed, destroying about twenty-eight thousand buildings
1939	World War II begins
2005	Hurricane Katrina floods New Orleans, killing about 1,800 people and causing an estimated $161 billion in damage
2020	The World Health Organization declares the COVID-19 outbreak a pandemic

Bibliography

*Books for young readers

"The Carolina Algonquian." National Park Service. Last updated
September 22, 2016. https://www.nps.gov/articles/
carolinaalgonquian.htm.

Emery, Theo. "The Roanoke Island Colony: Lost, and Found?"
New York Times, August 10, 2015. https://www.nytimes.com/
2015/08/11/science/the-roanoke-colonists-lost-and-found.
html.

*Fritz, Jean. ***The Lost Colony of Roanoke***. New York: Putnam, 2004.

Horn, James. ***A Kingdom Strange: The Brief and Tragic History of
the Lost Colony of Roanoke***. New York: Basic Books, 2010.

Kupperman, Karen Ordahl. ***Roanoke: The Abandoned Colony***.
Lanham, MD: Rowman & Littlefield Publishers, Inc., 2007.

Lawler, Andrew. "Is This Inscribed Stone a Notorious Forgery—or the
Answer to America's Oldest Mystery?" National Geographic,
June 2018, accessed September 20, 2023. https://www.
nationalgeographic.com/history/article/lost-colony-roanoke-
virginia-eleanor-dare-stone-mystery?.

Lawler, Andrew. *The Secret Token: Myth, Obsession, and the Search for the Lost Colony of Roanoke*. New York: Doubleday, 2018.

Miller, Lee. *Roanoke: Solving the Mystery of the Lost Colony*. New York: Arcade Publishing, 2001.

*Peterson, Megan Cooley. *The Lost Roanoke Colony*. North Mankato, MN: Capstone Press, 2022.

*Stemple, Heidi E. Y., and Jane Yolen. *Roanoke: The Lost Colony: An Unsolved Mystery from History*. New York: Simon & Schuster, 2003.

"Tribal History." Algonquian Indians of North Carolina, Inc. http://www.ncalgonquians.com/tribalhistory.html.